Steam in the North East

A Photo-Recollection of the 1950s' railway scene
by Ron Goult

Dalesman Books
1982

The Dalesman Publishing Company Ltd.,
Clapham, via Lancaster, LA2 8EB.
First published 1982

ISBN: 0 85206 700 3

Printed in Great Britain by Fretwell & Brian Ltd.,
Healey Works, Goulbourne Street, Keighley, West Yorkshire

Contents

Introduction 5
Express Passenger Trains 8
Semi-Fast Workings 18
Branch Lines 34
Freight Traffic 48
Locomotives of Yesteryear 69
Electric Stock 70

Front cover photograph of A3 No. 60084 *Trigo* departing from Leeds City with the North Briton by Eric Treacy.
The back cover photograph by the author depicts J77 68408 at Darlington shed yard in 1955.

Controversially rebuilt from Gresley's original A1, *Great Northern,* Thompson pacific A1/1 No. 60113 passes Selby with a parcels train. This design was later developed by Peppercorn into the very successful A1 class.

Introduction

IN producing this book I have tried to capture the railway scene as it really was in those halcyon days when the sight of a main-line diesel-electric locomotive – and there were six of them, the two LMS twins 10000 and 10001 and the Southern trio plus of course the solitary Fell mechanical which made spasmodic interesting appearances – was received with polite interest.

The rail enthusiast of the 1950s ranged from the young spotter, possibly aged about 9 years old with a pencil and loco-shed book, to the dedicated enthusiast of three score years and ten or more who readily recalled the pre-grouping era and who had still not really accepted nationalisation. No matter where one fitted in between these two ends of the scale, the thought that one day it would all be nothing more than a memory was inconceivable. But time moves on, and as we look back on the scene of twenty-five years ago I hope that this selection of photographs from my travels during the 1950s will evoke a few pleasant nostalgic memories of an era which is sadly missed by many.

The age of steam produced many individual ambitious projects, but the author never heard of anyone who managed to 'cop' every single locomotive although many tried. I must confess that at one time I did feel that it might be possible to photograph one representative of each of the 450–500 classes of locomotives in existence at that particular time. It must be remembered that in the pre-Beeching years there were hundreds of branch lines, many of which seemed to have a permanent allocation of some old locomotive working out its final years and giving the impression it could go on forever. I have deliberately refrained, except in the case of the picture of *The Great Marquess,* from selecting pictures of locomotives in pristine condition because in reality, unless a locomotive had just been outshopped after overhaul, they nearly all sported the same livery – a kind of grimy grey or black! Admittedly, selected locomotives which were selected to haul prestige trains like the Elizabethan illustrated on page 12 were turned out in a presentable condition, but unless a loco was being used on a Royal Train duty it was highly unlikely that it would be in service in the excellent condition which one can see in the preservation scene of to-day.

Many readers will recall another ritual which has now receded into the past – the inevitable shed trips. Whether it was a loco-spotters' outing or a visit organised by one of the societies, it meant the same thing, the visitation of possibly up to eight or more motive power depots in one day, usually a Sunday, when there were more locos 'on shed'. I can recall the sense of anticipation of what a particular depot may have had hidden behind its brick walls or rotting fence and the possibility of a bonus of some 'foreign' loco maintained interest right to the end. One often wonders how many miles were walked up and down between silent locomotives in 'straight sheds' dodging the inspection pits, open holes, pools of oily water and pieces of dismantled valve gear, but how enthralling it all was. Incidentally, to the uninitiated a 'straight shed' was one in which tracks were parallel to each other compared to a round house where the storage roads radiated out from a central turntable – the National Railway Museum at York is a typical example of the latter.

As a railway enthusiast the writer spent many hours at the lineside and on station platforms. I feel that many like myself will have some memories of visiting a small signal box in a remote spot and being welcomed by a friendly signalman who was only too pleased to chat and proudly demonstrate the workings of the box in his charge – shades of Eryholme Junction, Ais Gill and Scout Green. One of the most sadly missed aspects of the past is the great variety of motive power which one could see at any of the principal locations. In this respect the North Eastern Region was one of the most prolific, having the benefit of many long-serving elderly pre-grouping designs such as the Raven B16s and Q6s, the Worsdell J27s and D20s, several classes of Pacifics plus the pre-nationalisation designs of Thompson like the B1 and K1. British Railways designed locomotives were not too common on the North Eastern Region due to the fact that the ex LNER motive power stock covered most requirements so satisfactorily. The only area where a significant inroad was made was the displacement of the Raven Q7s and rebuilt O1s on the Tyne Dock–Consett line by one of B.R.s most successful designs, the Class 9F heavy freight locomotive.

One other interesting part of the fifties railway scene was that of coaching stock. Once one left the main line environment where the East Coast expresses speeded along with their uniform rakes of BR Standard Mk 1 stock, which was sometimes broken up by the inclusion of Thompson stock or the odd Gresley Buffet or Restaurant Car, the scene became more varied. Most semi-fast and branch line trains were composed of ex LNER and ex NER coaches, although the presence of some Great Central matchboard stock in the Darlington area added variety. The cascade policy of using redundant main line stock on secondary duties meant that the semi-fast expresses from Newcastle to Middlesbrough and Carlisle had the benefit of very comfortable accommodation. On the lesser branches radiating from Hull, Darlington and Newcastle it was not unusual for a train to include at least one vintage coach or even be formed of a whole rake of clerestory stock. One result of the availability of a wide variety of rolling stock was that, in addition to being able hastily to provide extra trains when required, the enthusiast could sometimes witness trains made up in such a way that nearly every coach would be of a different origin. With liveries of carmine and cream, carmine only and ex LNER teak, a real collection of allsorts would result.

In concluding this introduction in which I have recalled some of my personal memories of the pleasure of being a railway enthusiast in the fifties, I hope my reminiscences and the photographs contained in this book will evoke some nostalgic thoughts among readers and help them to relive, if only in thought, that wonderful age which gave so much pleasure to so many.

A8 69891 entering Ormesby with a Middlesbrough to Whitby train in June 1954.

Express Passenger Trains

EXPRESS passenger traffic in the North Eastern Region remained the province of the LNER Pacifics until their final demise in 1966, the pride of place being held until nearly the end by the Gresley designed streamlined A4s or 'Streaks' as they were affectionately known.

As has been stated previously, at the time of nationalisation the LNER possessed such a wide range of motive power of all categories that the new British Railways designs were superfluous to its requirements (with the exception of the ex Great Eastern section) and made very little impact on its operation. When one considers that at nationalisation the LNER handed over 112 tried and tested Gresley Pacifics plus another 50 in the form of the post-war designed and much underrated Peppercorn A1s, the operating department were certainly not short of express haulage power. In addition, there were 15 A2 Pacifics, also designed by Peppercorn, plus the varied but not so popular assortment of Thompson designs and rebuilds which brought the total Pacific strength to 202.

The top link duties usually fell to the A4s and A1s, the prestige Capitals Limited and Elizabethan being the prerogative of the A4s due to some of the class having corridor tenders which enabled a change of crew to take place enroute without stopping. The less exacting duties were often entrusted to the aging but reliable A3s which enjoyed a fresh lease of life towards the end. Many were then fitted with German type smoke deflectors in addition to the double chimneys added a few years earlier, giving them a new and imposing front end appearance. The other express duties which did not demand such high speed running, such as the inter-regional trains like the Newcastle to Liverpool and Bristol and the many Saturdays only relief workings, were handled by the A2s with support from the mixed traffic V2s, both of these classes being equally at home on express freights and parcels workings.

In contrast with the present day and the many complaints about overcrowding on the East Coast main line and the inflexibility of the HST stock, the expresses of a quarter of a century ago may have taken a longer time to complete their journeys but the average passenger could at least travel in the comfort of three-a-side seating with arm rests.

A3 60060 *The Tetrarch* climbs from the Stockton line to enter Northallerton with a Newcastle to Liverpool express in August 1955.

The up Queens of Scots Pullman races south through Northallerton headed by A3 No. 60036 *Colombo.* This train provided a more leisurely journey between London and the North being routed via Leeds.

A3 60036 *Colombo* hauling a Leeds to Newcastle express passing North-allerton on the low-level lines. As this locomotive was allocated to Leeds (Neville Hill), this working probably formed the outward leg of the turn on which it returned hauling the Pullman as shown in the photograph above.

After a heavy snowfall A3 60073 *St. Gatien* passes Manors near Newcastle with an Edinburgh to King's Cross express in December 1956.

A3 60072 *Sunstar* entering Stockton with the mid-morning Newcastle to Liverpool express. There were two of these daily which ran via Sunderland and the coast.

The down Elizabethan rounds the curve approaching Croft Spa headed by A4 60009 *Union of South Africa* which is now enjoying a new lease of life and is a regular performer on steam hauled excursions in Scotland.

A4 60011 *Empire of India* passing Selby with a King's Cross to Edinburgh express in September 1954. The reversed headboard is due to the fact that this was the Saturday equivalent of the Monday to Fridays only non-stop Elizabethan.

A2 60533 *Happy Knight* approaching Darlington (Bank Top) with a Newcastle – Liverpool express on 7th July, 1955. These locomotives were introduced in November 1947 and were Peppercorn's first design; only one of the class was completed before nationalisation on 1st January, 1948.

The last pre-nationalisation designed Pacific locomotives were the A1s, and here waiting for its next turn of duty is 60118 *Archibald Sturrock* in York yard.

Doncaster, one of the most popular locations for railfans. A1 60150 *Willbrook* heads south hauling the up Flying Scotsman on 5th June, 1954.

A Saturday morning relief Newcastle to King's Cross via Sunderland express approaching Eaglescliffe headed by A2/3 60511 *Airborne.* On a Summer Saturday one could observe many extra workings to the south at this location as trains were provided for the extra traffic generated by the large industrial areas of Wearside and Teesside.

Passing Darlington shed in the late afternoon, A2/3 60511 *Airborne* approaches Bank Top station with an Edinburgh to King's Cross express in August 1955.

Designed by Nigel Gresley in 1936 for express freight working, the V2 proved to be one of the most versatile locomotives in the country. Several were lent to the Southern Region in the early '50s and worked the Bournemouth Belle when the Southern's Pacifics were temporarily withdrawn with axle problems. Here 60853 heads an empty stock train through Selby on 5th June, 1954.

V2 60847 *St. Peter's School, York, A.D.627* and B16/3 61449 provide 'super power' for a York to King's Cross relief, photographed at Chaloners Whin Junction, York, on a summer Saturday in 1956.

V2 60873 standing outside Heaton shed.

Semi-Fast Workings

THE semi-fast trains of the fifties provided the all important services to the intermediate places which the expresses passed through at speed en route. Covering all the main lines and also forming some useful connecting links, they were generally in the hands of the B1 and B16 4–6–0s and 4–4–0 D49s. Although Middlesbrough to Newcastle trains via the coast were often referred to as expresses, they fall more into the above classification and were for many years in the sole hands of the V1 and V3 2–6–2 tank locomotives hauling sets of ex main line Gresley corridor stock.

Ex main line stock was also found on other semi-fast workings but many of the trains in the Leeds, Doncaster and Hull areas were composed of suburban stock. In those days there were many trains which only ran once daily and in some cases the only explanation for them could be that they were remnants of services which had been instituted for specific reasons many years ago and had remained unchanged over the years. One such working was a daily train which left Middlesbrough at lunchtime for Northallerton. Most of the duties referred to in this section quickly became victims of the mass dieselisation of the late 1950s.

One of the once very familiar B1 Class, 61288, hauling an up train through Selby.

After recent overhaul at the works, B17 61609 *Quidenham* arrives back at Doncaster with a stopping train from Leeds. As these locomotives were principally used on the Great Eastern section, this train was no doubt a running-in turn and provided an unusual 'cop' for the attendant train spotters.

In 1924 Gresley introduced the K3. One of its principal duties was on the overnight fish trains from Scotland to the south but in later years it became a very useful general purpose locomotive. 61897 is seen passing Great Coates near Grimsby with a Bank Holiday Monday excursion to Cleethorpes in 1959.

When taking railway photographs the photographer cannot always have the lighting as he would wish and sometimes the result is a picture which is full of contrast. This view taken against the setting sun is of B1 61224 coasting into Malton with a York to Scarborough train on 4th April, 1954.

K1 62064 entering Middlesbrough with a football special from Bishop Auckland.

B16/1 61478 waiting to depart from Eaglescliffe with a very varied assortment of coaching stock bound for Newcastle.

In 1937 Gresley rebuilt several of the Raven B16s incorporating outside valve gear and a modified footplating. The photograph shows B16/2 61457 pounding through Selby with a through train from Lowestoft to York on 5th June, 1954.

On 2nd September, 1956, B16/1 No. 61443 was turned out in ex-works condition to haul the Tees Tyne Rail Tour and is seen here during a photographic halt. The tour which had originated in the Manchester area had been hauled to Darlington by a 'Britannia', possibly the first to visit the area.

The same train at Wellfield.

Another Raven B16/1, 61456, arrives at Scarborough with a train from York in August 1953.

In the southern part of the area were several ex Great Central designs. Prominent among these around the Sheffield area were the D11s. In the photograph 62664 *Princess Mary* is about to depart from Manchester Central in June 1955.

The last D10 62653 *Sir Edward Fraser* standing in Northwich shed in 1955.

Grouped around the turntable in Borough Gardens shed are B1 61320, J71 68289, and J72 68705, taken in November 1953.

D49/2 62766 *The Grafton* passing Brough with a Leeds to Hull train in September 1954.

One of the first classes to feel the impact of dieselisation was the D49s which were used on the lightly loaded semi-fast passenger trains around the York area. D49/2 62726 *The Meynell* was photographed at Scarborough one Sunday morning in 1954.

D49/2 62741 *The Blankley* leaving Hull with a train for Leeds in September 1954.

Pressed into passenger service, J39 64982 arrives at Middlesbrough with a football special from West Auckland.

In the early fifties, Northallerton had a small allocation of D20s which used to work the Wensleydale branch and were regular performers on a turn to Middlesbrough. The photograph shows D20/1 62347 entering Thornaby with a Middlesbrough to Northallerton train on 29th May, 1954.

Another class to fall early victim to the DMUs were the V3s on the Middlesbrough to Newcastle line. 67691 is seen entering Middlesbrough in 1954.

Enveloped in steam, A8 69876 pulls out of Stockton with a Newcastle train. The overall station roof seen in the background has now been removed.

Pressed into service on passenger working WD 90430 pulls out of Hull Paragon for Boothferry Park on a football special in September 1954.

Ex L.M.S. Class 4MT leaving Hull Paragon with a football special for Boothferry Park in September 1954.

J52 68875 standing at the down platform at Doncaster while acting as station pilot in June 1954.

Branch Lines

IN many respects the branch line of the fifties played a very important part in the structure of the railway system and could be looked at in different ways. Firstly it was a feeder to the main line, thus providing a railway service for the millions of the population who do not happen to live in a town situated on a main line. In this respect it also meant freight services could be provided to places miles away from the main centres; unfortunately many of these have been withdrawn and the lost traffic transferred to road haulage. A second function of the branch line which is more relevant than ever today is its use for commuting; in areas where branch lines have managed to survive they usually provide cheaper and quicker services than the equivalent bus. With the general trend of people tending to move out of the towns and the necessity of daily commuting it is a great pity that lack of foresight in the late fifties has denied the travelling public of many services which would have been well patronised today.

In the North East the natural motive on the branch lines was the tank locomotive. The large pre-grouping Pacific types such as the A5 and A8, ably assisted by the Gresley V3s and the new Thompson L1s, took care of the more heavily loaded branch line trains and also some of the lighter services which travelled some of the steeply graded routes in the North Yorkshire area. In the early fifties the faithful 0–4–4 G5s were still giving valiant service on the lighter trains and the 0–6–0 J21s monopolised the testing route to Kirkby Stephen over Stainmore. Both these classes were later replaced by Standard 2–6–2 tank locomotives which appeared on the scene at the latter end of the period. Like the trains referred to in the previous section all succumbed to the inevitable DMU if the branch managed to escape the Beeching axe.

Originally built as 4–4–4 tank locomotives between 1913 and 1922, these locomotives were rebuilt by Gresley in the 1930s with a 4–6–2 wheel arrangement to give better tractive effort. They were used in most areas of the North East and in this photograph 69859 is seen climbing up the 1 in 40 bank to enter Ormesby station with a Middlesbrough to Whitby train in June 1953.

A8 69886 waiting to leave Brough with a stopping train for Hull in September 1954.

Hauling some rather vintage stock, A8 69880 coasts down the bank into Ormesby with an Esk Valley train bound for Middlesbrough in June 1953.

The A5/2 class were built by the L.N.E.R. in 1925 with mountings and cab profile reduced to suit the loading gauge and were a modified design of the A5/1 introduced by the Great Central in 1911. The locomotive in the photograph is pulling away from Cargo Fleet with a Saltburn to Darlington stopping train on 3rd November, 1953.

After overhaul at Darlington Works, this A5/1 of Great Central design was photographed at Middlesbrough on a running-in turn. Note the difference between this locomotive and the cut-down version shown above.

About to enter Falsgrave Tunnel, Scarborough, the driver of B1 61062 receives the tablet before setting off with a train for Whitby in August 1953.

Last stronghold of the long serving D20s was the Alnmouth and Alnwick workings to Newcastle. Here 62383 waits at Newcastle Central with a return working in October 1956.

One D20 was rebuilt in 1941 with modified footplating. D20/2 62349 is seen at Carlisle on 27th June, 1953.

Standing inside Hull (Botanic Gardens) shed are two C12 tank locomotives, 67391 and 67397. These engines were more usually seen in the Barnsley, Sheffield and Doncaster areas, being of Great Northern design.

Four of the Thompson designed L1 2–6–4 tank locomotives were on the usual allocation of Darlington shed and were regular performers on the Saltburn and Richmond branches. Here 67777 takes water before working its next turn of duty.

L1 67750 departing from Cargo Fleet with a train for Darlington in April 1954. This usual six coach formation has now been replaced by a two-car DMU.

The most numerous class of 0–4–4 tank locomotive possessed by the L.N.E.R. was the G5. Built around the turn of the century, all were in service at nationalisation nearly fifty years later and provided the backbone of the services on lightly loaded branch lines. 67280 is seen here about to enter Brough to form a return working to Hull. Several of these locomotives, this one among them, were fitted for push-pull working.

One of the first classes to be displaced by DMUs were the N1s, which were regular performers on the Leeds to Bradford trains. Here, shortly before being withdrawn, 69459 waits to leave Leeds Central.

Resting in the yard of its home shed, G5 67240 at Whitby.

Taken in the 1960s this photograph of Gresley designed K4 3442 *The Great Marquess* at Grassington shows how resplendent a locomotive can look given the right care and attention.

Fairburn 2–6–4 tank 42084 arriving at Darlington with a Sunday train from Saltburn. Due to engineering works near Dinsdale the train had been diverted over the Fighting Cocks branch; hence its arrival from a northerly direction in May 1955.

One of the last classes of steam locomotive to be built at Swindon Works, Standard Class 3MT No. 77003 enters Middlesbrough with a train for Saltburn on 12th June, 1954.

Waiting in the bay at Northallerton in June 1956 is ex L.M.S. Class 2MT 46474 with the daily Wensleydale parcels train. Until April 1954 a passenger service operated to Garsdale but after this was withdrawn the branch was gradually cut back and now exists only as far as Redmire.

A Standard Class 3MT tank waits to leave Darlington with a train for Richmond in September 1955.

When the J21s were being withdrawn from service in the Darlington area, the Darlington to Penrith trains over the Stainmore Summit route were taken over by Standard Class 3MT tank locos. Here we see 82026 approaching Piercebridge with a train for Penrith.

Another lightly loaded working which proved suitable for the region's newly acquired class 3MT tanks was that from Darlington to Richmond. Here a return working from Richmond is seen approaching Croft Spa on 14th July, 1955.

Freight Traffic

THE railways in the North East evolved due to the requirement to move hundreds of tons of coal, iron ore, and all the other materials associated with heavy industry, throughout the region and to other parts of the country. Although many lines closed over the years and were lifted, heavy freight was very prominent in the fifties and still persists today. One could witness a daily procession of freight trains, sometimes running nose to tail, in the industrial area around Teesside. Three classes of locomotive virtually monopolised these workings, the ex NER J26s and Q6s and the ex W.D. 2–8–0's, all of which rendered yeoman service – in fact the last steam workings in the North Eastern Region were performed by the pre-grouping types. Further north the areas of Tyne & Wear were also served by J27s and Q6s with the freight-only Tyne Dock to Consett line in the hands of the three cylinder Q7s assisted by Ex Great Central rebuilt O1s. It was this line which during its latter years saw the main intrusion into the ex LNER power stronghold when the BR Standard 9F 2–10–0s took over the heavy ore trains; this necessitated fitting the locomotives with air pumps to operate the doors on the special ore wagons.

Away from the coal areas of Northumberland and Durham, freight workings tended to be placed in the hands of Thompson K1s, B1s and ex NER B16s. The Pennine line to Kirkby Stephen carried a significant freight traffic for many years between Furness and Workington, the West Coast route and the South Durham areas. Due to weight limitations over the various viaducts, motive power was restricted to ancient J25 0–6–0s which usually required a sister engine for rear-end assistance. Eventually these classes were replaced by ex LMS 2MT Moguls before all freight traffic was rerouted via Carlisle and Newcastle involving a considerable increase in mileage.

A great deal of traffic from the South Yorkshire area was worked as far as York by locomotives from that district and consequently many of the heavy 2–8–0 classes could be seen heading past Chaloners Whin Junction. Even LMS Beyer Garretts from the Nottingham area were not a rare sight.

Sharing the freight duties on Teesside with the Q6s were the J26 and J27 classes. Here J26 65776 is seen passing Cargo Fleet in 1953 with a train of hopper wagons closely followed by a sister engine on a similar working.

An unidentified J27 hauling a freight train near Pelaw on the line from Tyne Dock in 1956.

J26 65746 passing through Middlesbrough on the goods lines with an eastbound freight in July 1955.

J26 65745 passing one of her predecessors, J25 65720, at Cargo Fleet in March 1959.

B16/1 61447 heads south through Croft Spa with a mixed freight on 14th July, 1955. Introduced by Raven in 1920, these locomotives of North Eastern design lasted well into B.R. days, most of the class being allocated to York.

Mainstay of the heavy freight on Teesside, Q6 63430 drifts down the bank at Ormesby with a train from Skinningrove Iron Works in June 1954.

Q6 63354 photographed at Borough Gardens in 1954.

Waiting between duties, J21 65064 stands at Kirkby Stephen. For many years these locomotives, which were introduced in 1886, together with their sister engine the J25, were the main motive power for the heavily graded route over the Pennines from Barnard Castle to Kirkby Stephen. The last of the class survived until April 1962.

In 1919 the North Eastern introduced a heavy freight locomotive designed by Raven. Having three cylinders, it was more powerful than its more numerous predecessor, the Q6, and was classified T3 later to become Q7. Its most frequent use was on the heavy ore trains on the Tyne Dock to Consett line, but on this occasion we see 63460 passing Darlington on an up freight in 1955. Fortunately one of the class has been preserved.

The other class of locomotive usually associated with the Tyne Dock line was the O1 which was introduced in 1944 and was a Thompson rebuild of Robinson's Great Central O4s. The majority of these were to be found in the Doncaster and Sheffield area. The photograph shows No. 63863.

When the Q7s and O1s were displaced from Tyne Dock, their Consett workings were taken over by the powerful Standard 9Fs. Here 92061 pulls up the incline from Tyne Dock quay assisted at the rear by a J25.

Q7 63470 preparing to work an afternoon freight at Pelaw.

An ex R.O.D. locomotive classified as 04/3 at Frodingham.

Heavy freight locomotives from the South Yorkshire area regularly worked into York where this O2/2 63943 was photographed.

J10 65175, taken in 1954.

A wintry scene at Newcastle as A2/3 60515 *Sun Stream* negotiates the pointwork at the east end of the station in December 1956.

In 1949 Peppercorn introduced the K1 Class Mogul. This was developed from Thompson's K1/1 design which was a rebuild of one of Gresley's K4s which were introduced in 1937 for work on the West Highland line. The K1s were a very useful mixed traffic loco and were often used on freight trains in the North East. 62005, seen here in Darlington shed yard in June 1955, has now been restored to L.N.E.R. livery and preserved in working order.

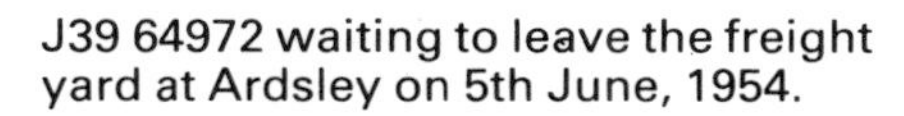
J39 64972 waiting to leave the freight yard at Ardsley on 5th June, 1954.

The Gresley K3s were not a very common sight in the North East but one could observe them on odd occasions. Here 61945 hauls a very lightweight freight through Selby in September 1954.

Typical of the thrifty attitude of the LNER towards design costs is the fact that the J72 design of Wilson Worsdell, introduced in 1898, was considered so satisfactory that further batches of the same design were built in the 1920s and in 1949 after nationalisation. The photograph shows 69021, which was built as recently as 1951, in Darlington shed yard.

After being withdrawn from service, S1 tank 69902 awaits scrapping at Darlington in 1956.

Worsdell's earliest design of 0–6–2 tank was the N8. These were introduced in 1886, the last one being withdrawn in October 1956 thus spanning a period of seventy years. One of the class is seen in Tyne Dock shed in 1954.

Another heavy tank locomotive used primarily for shunting was the 4–8–0 class T1 introduced by Worsdell in 1909. Most of these were allocated to sheds in the Teesside area but two were used at Tyne Dock where 69920 was photographed in 1953.

At the beginning of the century Worsdell added the N10 to his previous 0–6–2 tank loco designs. These had smaller diameter wheels but slightly larger bunkers than their predecessors. Towards the end of their lives most of the class worked in the Hull area; the photograph shows 69093 at Dairycoates in 1954.

In 1910 Raven designed a heavy tank loco for short haul freight workings. Twenty were built and became class A7. Most of them were used in the Hull area; the photograph shows 69783 at Springhead in April 1954.

Designed for the Great Central by Robinson in 1906, these small dock tanks became LNER class J63 and spent most of their later years at Immingham Dock where 68204 was photographed in 1953.

A later design of 0–6–0 was the J94, built during the Second World War for the Ministry of Supply. Many were acquired by the L.N.E.R. in 1946 and put to good use in shunting and trip working duties. 68050 was photographed at Darlington in 1954.

Shortly after its withdrawal from banking duties on the Lickey Incline, the only ex L.N.E.R. Garrett was at Gorton prior to being scrapped. No. 69999 is seen here in 1955.

Rebuilt in the 1940s from ex Great Central design Q4s, the Q1s were mostly confined to shunting duties – two were allocated to Selby. The photograph shows 69932 at Frodingham in 1954. Some of the class carried an oval-shaped totem on the bunker sides displaying the intitials L.N.E.R.

WD 90074 slowly passes through Eaglescliffe with a South-bound freight in October 1954.

WD 90081 passing Croft Spa with an up freight in July 1955.

A Sunday morning shot at Hull Springhead shed of two WDs 90094 and 90586 on 4th April, 1954.

A mixed freight passing Eaglescliffe hauled by WD 90014. The buildings in the background have now been replaced by an island platform and bus-stop type shelter.

WD 90704 and K3 61874 under the coaling plant at Hull Dairycoates on April 4th, 1954.

For a short time Northallerton had an allocation of the new Standard class 2 2–6–0s. Here 78010 stands at the entrance to the small yard in August 1956.

Locomotives of Yesteryear

The once familiar view at Darlington Bank Top station of former Stockton & Darlington locomotive *Derwent*. This locomotive has since been moved to North Road station for permanent exhibition.

On the weekend of 19th September, 1953, Doncaster works held an open day. Among the locomotives on view was the famous Stirling Single No. 1.

Electric Stock

(Ex L.N.E.R.)

IT was felt that it would not be unreasonable to include a short section about ex NER and LNER electric traction in this book. In 1903 the North Eastern Railway decided something had to be done to compete with the new electric tramways which were taking traffic from the local rail network in the North Tyneside area. Its answer was to electrify a near circular route which reached Whitley Bay in the east and returned to Newcastle, making it one of the first large cities to have an electric suburban service. Later in the 1930s it was decided to electrify the lines south of the Tyne to Jarrow and South Shields, and on completion of this scheme the North Tyneside stock was transferred to it. North Tyneside in turn received an entirely new fleet of articulated units.

In 1915 the NER with a view to future electrification put overhead wiring on the mineral line from Shildon to the vast marshalling yards at Newport south of the Tees, and with the experience gained from the scheme put forward proposals to elelctrify the main line from Newcastle to York. Although one locomotive was built for this venture, the scheme was lost due to the grouping of 1923.

Main line electrification ideas lay dormant until the late 1930s when Gresley designed a locomotive with ideas for the future. Unfortunately the war prevented any further progress until 1954 when the heavily graded ex Great Central line over the Pennines was electrified from Manchester to Sheffield with a branch to Wath from Dunford Bridge for freight working. Fifty-seven Bo-Bo locomotives were built to operate the line, based on a modified version of the original LNER design which was also taken into the running stock. In 1954 an additional seven locomotives of Co-Co wheel arrangement were introduced to handle passenger trains. In 1981 the decision was taken to close this particular route and so the last remnants of the LNER's electrifications disappeared.

Originally introduced for North Tyneside electrification these units were transferred to the South Tyneside system in 1934 and worked on that system till the whole of the electric network was abandoned in favour of DMUs in 1967. The train in the photograph is arriving at Newcastle from South Shields in 1955.

Built in 1938 to take over from the older stock on the North Tyneside system, these units were of articulated formation and of very modern design. This train working the circular route is passing Manors; the tramway type overhead wiring on the right hand side of the photograph is for the Quayside branch locomotives.

Introduced specially in 1954 for working passenger trains between Manchester and Sheffield via Woodhead was class EM2 Co-Co. 27000, seen here at Reddish Depot, was the first of a class of seven locomotives.

Also photographed at Reddish the same day was the original class EM1 locomotive, 26000, named *Tommy.* Built in 1941, it was lent to the Netherlands Railways for evaluation after the end of World War II and was so christened by the Dutch railwaymen.